# Hunting, Gathering, & Videogames

First edition published in 1999 by The Graduate Group under the title *Why Do We Have to Work? A Search for Understanding, Peace of Mind, and an Alternative Measure of Success.* Second edition published in 2003 by Virtualbookworm.com Publishing, Inc. under the title *Why Do We Have to Work?* Third edition, under the title *Hunting, Gathering, & Videogames,* was published in 2005 by Heliographica.

Printed in the United States of America.

Booklocker.com, Inc.
2006

# Hunting, Gathering, & Videogames

## Todd Allen Gates

*To Dustin, Jesse, Tyler, and Roxanna*

# Acknowledgments

My gratitude to those who read drafts of this book and improved it with their edits and comments: Chris Adams, Rolls Andre, Kathleen Bulgreen, Melton Cartes, Kathleen D. Gallagher, George Gates, Wendy Gates, Martha Kamber, Tim Marback, Blaine Palmer, Rick Rodstrom, John Sullivan, Arthur Thexton, Nina West, Bob Whitman, and Mara Whitman.

# CONTENTS

# Introduction

When I was a teenager, my friends and I harshly criticized the adult world's preoccupation with money. The pursuit of wealth seemed to overshadow everything important in life, and for *what*? This abstract thing called money has no apparent inherent value: you can't eat it, wear it, or do anything very useful with it in its bare form. We understood that money was necessary if one wanted food, clothing and shelter, but didn't understand why these basics had to be bought and sold. I don't remember spending much time pondering over the place of finance in my life, other than sharing with my peers an indifference to what we referred to as "only money."

My monetary ignorance did me little harm during my first several years as an independent adult: my income as a musician was admittedly sporadic at best, but supplementary money from waiting tables allowed me to get by. Once I got married and became a father, however, my lifestyle no longer worked very well. I was unprepared for what should have been predictable expenses, and found myself overwhelmed with financial problems.

In addition to my anxieties about money, I was also discovering that my all-consuming dedication to my music was no longer compatible with having a happy life. Prior to fatherhood it had always made sense to give my career 100%: without thinking about it in exactly such terms, I had been following our culture's guideline that a career determines your identity, or "who you are." This guideline created a lot of personal conflicts once I became a parent. When I tried to continue my normal schedule of spending long nights out with my band practicing, performing, or recording, I began to have regrets: I felt I was heading for a distant relationship with my son, and a divorce from my wife, who was stuck with most of the child-rearing. And when I spent prolonged periods of time with my new family, I felt preoccupied and restless: how could I succeed in a field as competitive as music without giving it my all? Pursuing happiness and identity through my occupation was the only path I had ever considered, but suddenly this path was giving me nothing but stress.

Now, I had an easier time than many other musicians I know who have also contemplated switching careers. First of all, music was bringing in hardly any money: it wasn't like I had to figure out what else could earn me such a huge salary. Second, I didn't possess such an overwhelming talent that the musical loss to the world had to be considered. But once I made the decision to put music on hold, I began asking myself the questions that eventually led me to write this book. If having time for my family meant finding a career that I wouldn't be *too* personally committed to, yet I still internalized the notion that my occupation defined the essence of who I was, what kind of work could satisfy such contradictory goals? What role should a job have in my life? *Why do we have to work anyway?* Sources from several different fields—anthropology, economics, social criticism, self-help—gave me pieces of the answer, and this book is the result of tying those pieces together.

## PART I: WHY DO WE HAVE TO WORK?

### Chapter One
*Hunting, Gathering, & Videogames* gives a historical overview of why we've *always* had to "go to work," tracing the common link between the workday of the prehistoric hunter and gatherer, the first millennium B.C. farmer, the first century A.D. pottery-maker, the nineteenth century assembly line worker, and today's videogame programmer.

### Chapter Two
*Surgery & Dental Floss* spells out the complications of bartering, and explains why communities with multiple goods and services always end up using some form of money (be it beads or dollar bills) to solve their trading problems.

## Chapter Three

*Penguins & Peacocks* is about why the changes in our workday—the transition from hunting and gathering to the ages of agriculture, industry, and information—took place, even though some aspects of these changes were for the worse. It looks at the parallel between the history of our workday and the way evolution works in nature: how change is driven by the demands of the immediate environment, not by concerns for future repercussions.

## PART II: WORK, WEALTH, & HAPPINESS

## Chapter Four

*Emperors & Emptiness* gives an overview of three drawbacks of our modern work system: the alienation, the perception of deprivation that can come from being in a society overflowing with goods and services, and the way our increased number of career options has opened up a large window for failure—particularly when we tie our occupation to our identity.

## Chapter Five

*More vs. Enough* offers an alternative to the unattainable American financial goal of "more is better" by outlining a flexible but precise definition of how much income is "enough."

## Chapter Six

*Measuring Success* contrasts our culture's guideline for happiness—the wealth, status, and identity we derive from our careers—with a guideline that instead aims for a balance of our physical, emotional, mental, and spiritual dimensions.

The insights I've gained from writing this book have helped me find (relative) peace within employment, and it's my hope they'll help the reader as well.

# PART I: WHY DO WE HAVE TO WORK?

# 1. Hunting, Gathering, & Videogames: the historical path of obtaining food, clothing and shelter

If we went back in time to live in the age of our prehistoric hunting and gathering ancestors, we would *still* have to go to work. For our food we'd have to hunt wild animals and gather plantlife, for protection from the climate we'd have to make clothing, and for shelter we'd need to build some kind of housing. An advantage to this way of life is that there would be no questions in our minds about why we were working: we would know it was about survival. A disadvantage is that most of us would not live very well—we'd have homes without heat, plumbing, or refrigerators; we'd have to deal with hungry cougars and mosquitoes without having the protection of rifles and insect repellent; and the threat of starvation would always lurk, particularly in the winter. But our early ancestors were unlikely to have felt deprived by the lack of such comforts, as they knew no lifestyle other than their own. So why the move from that straightforward "workday" to our current confusing world of office cubicles, rush hour train commutes, and stock market peaks and crashes?

The monumental step that took the human race away from the hunting and gathering life and into the age of agriculture, writes anthropologist Jared Diamond in *The Third Chimpanzee*, was probably accidental: discarded seeds were "planted" around home base, and people gradually began to notice the advantage of having some control over their food supply. Now, intentional planting might not be particularly important if you happened to live in an area where food was already plentiful. When a twentieth century hunter and gatherer of the Kalahari Desert Bushmen was once asked why his tribe didn't plant crops, he replied, "Why should we plant, when there are so many mongongo nuts in the world?"[i] For those areas without plenty of mongongo nuts (figuratively speaking), however, agriculture offers the great advantage of improving the chances

---

[i] Jared Diamond, *The Third Chimpanzee*, p. 184.

of securing your next meal. The same advantage explains the domestication of animals such as cows and sheep. This must have been a great motivating factor for people who, unlike most modern Americans, didn't take a food supply for granted.

If we had simply switched our workday from hunting and gathering to planting and herding, I would have no incentive to write this book. I wouldn't be concerned about my children ever asking me "Why do I have to work?"—the alternative of starvation would be obvious enough. But the purely practical developments of plant and animal domestication had repercussions that complicate the answer to this simple question.

Because agriculture is so much more efficient than hunting and gathering, it allows for great amounts of food to be produced by just a small segment of the population. This in turn allows others in the community to dedicate their lives to pursuits other than food collection. If it takes, say, only a quarter of the community to provide food for all the rest, the other three-quarters can then concentrate on a variety of specialized skills: tool making, astronomy, medicine, music, etc. The products of those specialized skills can then be traded for food. Agriculture, in other words, gives rise to specialists. It's agriculture's legacy that allowed the Mayans to create their calendar, scientists to develop vaccinations, and Nirvana to record *Nevermind*. Unlike the hunting and gathering days, a person's workday in an agricultural society might have nothing to do with directly providing his or her survival basics.

But if the agricultural system allows for just a small part of the population to provide the food, clothing and shelter for everyone else, then why does *everyone* have to work?

The answer is that we need either to create a product or to provide a service so we can engage in trade with the farmers, tailors, and shelter-builders (or shelter-renters, as the case may be). As self-interest is the motivating force behind almost every human action, it follows that nobody is going to put in the effort to harvest, sew, or build something and then let others just take it for free. If *we* were the farmers, would we put in all the extra hours necessary to create a surplus of crops if we weren't going to get anything in return? The ancient practice of barter is the logical next step once people become specialists.

Suppose you have only three people in a community. Suppose one person happens to excel at farming, another at carpentry, and the other at creating videogames. It's in the interest of each to specialize in his or her own area of expertise, produce a bit more than is personally needed, and then trade the surplus with the other two. This way all three will end up with good food, furniture, and videogames. [1]

The answer to "Why do I have to work?" in a small agricultural community is still fairly clear-cut: either you work the land for your food, or you have some kind of specialized skill that creates a product that can be traded for food. (It's probably no coincidence that the word *trade* means both *occupation* and *to exchange*.[ii]) But the connection between the modern workday and obtaining our survival basics isn't quite as direct. When seeking employment today, we're not looking to "make things" so we can barter with farmers and other specialists; we're looking for jobs that will provide us with a steady supply of either green paper in our hands or electronic numbers in our bank accounts (as well as providing us with, we hope, some sort of personal fulfillment). Our labor of course *does* provide for our survival, because we exchange our green paper and bank account numbers for our groceries, clothes and rent ... but it all seems unnecessarily complicated. How and why did this happen?

The answer became clearer to me after reading Alvin Toffler's *The Third Wave*, in which he explains how the transition from agriculture (or what Toffler calls the First Wave) to the Industrial Revolution (the Second Wave) contorted our once straightforward workday.

## The First Wave (8000 B.C. – A.D. 1600s)

The adoption of agriculture marked man's first turning point, or first new way of life. In addition to creating specialists, agriculture also led people to stop wandering in pursuit of game, and instead stay rooted to their

---

[ii] None of the etymology dictionaries I checked specifically confirmed this, but one could argue that the link is implied by the chronology behind the word's different meanings— 1546: the noun "one's business"; 1548: the verb form of that noun; 1555: "buying and selling"; late 1500s: "to exchange." (Sources: *The Oxford Dictionary of Word Histories*, and the *Online Etymology Dictionary* at www.geocities.com/etymonline/index.html.)

land—thus the creation of villages. Wherever agriculture arose, what we call "civilization" took root, whether in Africa, the Americas, Asia, Europe, or the Middle East. Despite cultural differences, there were similarities among all agricultural societies: divisions of labor, religions that became more or less organized, and some form of government. Depending on the degree to which labor could be specialized (details discussed in endnote 3), repercussions of the First Wave also included large populations, international trade, and accumulated knowledge through written records.[2]

## The Second Wave (1700s–1950s)

The aftermaths of the First Wave led to the Second Wave, the Industrial Revolution. This second turning point in human history began with the invention of machines that could replace human and animal strength. Another part of the upheaval was the degree to which labor was divided. Rather than the First Wave method of a specialist making a complete product one at a time, the Second Wave method was to divide the production up among multiple workers. This is where the workday gets more complicated, and starts to look more like our own.

Take the making of pins. In a small agricultural community, there would be a specialist dedicated to making one pin at a time. In Adam Smith's 1776 *The Wealth of Nations,* he describes the "new" pin-making process: "One man draws out the wire, another straightens it, a third cuts it, a fourth points it, a fifth grinds it at the top for receiving the head ..."[iii] Today's corporations have a parallel arrangement: each employee contributes a small part to the larger task of producing a company's product or service.

Why did this Second Wave occur—why would an agricultural society want to industrialize? After all, many of the changes associated with the Industrial Revolution are negative: pollution, ugly factories, mind-numbingly repetitive labor done by oppressed workers, rampant greed on the part of the factory owners, and destruction of the environment and traditional cultures. What motivated such a move?[3]

---

[iii] Adam Smith, *The Wealth of Nations*, Chapter 1, "Of the Division of Labour."

Industry's emergence may have been a "revolution," but what drove it was similar to what drove our distant human relatives some two million years earlier to sharpen their sticks and stones before going out to hunt. Sharpened weapons got the job done more reliably, so those capable of making such tools were the most likely to survive long enough to produce offspring. Likewise, planting did a more reliable job of securing food than did hunting and gathering, so those who adopted agriculture were the most likely to survive and reproduce. Survival also explains the adoption of industry: because goods produced via assembly lines and coal-powered machine strength were less expensive to make, they could be sold for less than handmade goods. To return to the change in the pin-making process—Adam Smith estimated that ten craftsmen, each making one pin at a time, would turn out a total of about 200 per day. Ten pin-factory workers each doing their own specialized task, however, could turn out over 48,000! So when it came to competition between the relatively expensive products from small shops vs. the inexpensive products from factories, it's no surprise that large industries had the greater "survival rate."

Car manufacturing provides another example of why the industrial methods, for better or worse, became widespread. In the beginning of the 1900s, automakers built the framework of their cars by having all the parts carried to a stationary assembly point, taking twelve and a half hours to finish the job. When Henry Ford started building cars using the assembly line method, the exact same job took only one and a half hours. As a result, Ford's cars were much more affordable than those of his competitors: Ford made it possible for the average person to own what was previously considered a luxury item. Just to keep their businesses alive, all other car manufacturers were forced to switch to using assembly lines as well.[4]

## The Third Wave (1950s–today)

In today's age of information, our labor is so precisely divided and specialized that many workers never deal directly with, and indeed may never even *see*, their company's product. An American employee in today's pin-manufacturing company would probably be involved in what's called "adding value" to the finished product, such as doing sales research (the actual pin-making is more likely to be done overseas where the labor is cheaper). There's of course much more to the computer age than just a refinement of the division of labor, but for the limited purposes of this chapter I'll go no further, and treat this Third Wave as only an extension of the Second.

This condensed history of our workday shows that the answer to the question "Why do I have to work?" is the same for the prehistoric hunter and gatherer, the first millennium B.C. farmer, the first century A.D. pottery-maker, the nineteenth century assembly line worker, and today's videogame programmer—each works to obtain food, clothing and shelter. The differences are only a matter of "how":

- the prehistoric method is by direct hunting, gathering, planting, sewing, and building;

- the First Wave method is by producing some good or providing some service that can be used for bartering (usually via currency, to be discussed in the next chapter) with herders, farmers, tailors, and carpenters;

- the Second/Third Wave method is by contributing to a *part* of the production of a good or service that can be traded (via currency) for the products that come from the food, clothing and shelter industries.

If we don't "go to work" by one of these three methods, our options for access to survival basics are unreliable,[iv] or at the very least, unattractive: stealing, gambling, begging, scavenging, or being dependent on family members, friends, or the government (welfare). These frequently have consequences that tend to run contrary to personal happiness: jail, hunger, poverty, and strained relationships with resentful friends and family.[5]

---

[iv] Exceptions are those who've accumulated or inherited enough money to live off the interest—but such people are rare, and unlikely to be part of this book's audience.

In the tribal love-rock musical *Hair*, the hippie leader Berger rejects the idea of needing a job, and sees no reason why he can't spend his life hanging out in the park, singing songs, taking drugs, and traveling with friends. But although he sees no reason why *he* should have to work, he apparently still wants *other* people to work, because he still wants the products of their labor: prepared food, clothing, drugs, and a car with a full tank of gas. His idea of freedom from work is hardly revolutionary—that kind of self-centered logic is embraced by every 3-year-old. Unless he can justify the position of "other people should labor to create things for me, and I shouldn't have to give them anything in return," his shunning of work just shows his confusion about our modern workday.

Of course, it may be that Berger is just a lazy freeloader. But even if that's the case, I believe that his type of attitude would be less common if our labor and our immediate survival were more directly linked. For suppose we were transported back in time several centuries, and to an area where we had to tend the crops for our food and build our own log cabins for shelter. If Berger were there, would he still feel justified in spending half his waking day playing in the woods, and spending the other half asking neighbors for food and shelter—figuring it's "only fair" since everyone else has so much, and he has so little? My guess is that he would not. Yet those who are inattentive to income in today's world are similar to those of yesteryear who were inattentive toward laboring for their food, clothing and shelter: the only difference is the roundabout route our labor now takes.

. . .

The adult world assumes that the answer to "Why do I have to work?" is obvious, and young people who question our system are more likely to be brushed off than given an accurate and satisfying explanation. I recently read the original story of *Pinocchio* to my children, and was struck by how little empathy Pinocchio's elders had for his naiveté—a naiveté that should have been expected from a dependent who had been alive for only a few days. Consider the following dialogue between Pinocchio and the Talking Cricket:

"I will not go," answered the Cricket, "until I have told you a great truth."

"Tell it to me then, and be quick about it."

"Woe to those boys who rebel against their parents, and run away capriciously from home. They will never come to any good in the world, and sooner or later they will repent bitterly."

"Sing away, Cricket, as you please, and as long as you please. For me, I have made up my mind to run away tomorrow at daybreak, because if I remain I shall not escape the fate of all other boys. I shall be sent to school and shall be made to study either by love or by force. To tell you in confidence, I have no wish to learn; it is much more amusing to run after butterflies, or to climb trees and to take the young birds out of their nests."

"Poor little goose! Do you not know that in that way you will grow up a perfect donkey, and that everyone will make game of you?"

"Hold your tongue, you wicked ill-omened croaker!" shouted Pinocchio.

But the Cricket, who was patient and philosophical, instead of becoming angry at this impertinence, continued in the same tone: "If you do not wish to go to school, why not at least learn a trade, if only to enable you to earn honestly a piece of bread."

"Do you want me to tell you?" replied Pinocchio, who was beginning to lose patience. "Among all the trades in the world there is only one that really takes my fancy."

"And that trade—what is it?"

"It is to eat, drink, sleep, and amuse myself, and to lead a vagabond life from morning to night."'

"As a rule," said the Talking Cricket with the same composure, "all those who follow that trade almost always end either in a hospital or in prison."

"Take care, you wicked ill-omened croaker! Woe to you if I fly into a passion!"[v]

[A few more words are exchanged, and the conversation ends abruptly after Pinocchio throws a hammer at the Talking Cricket, flattening him against the wall.]

---

[v] Carlo Collodi, *Pinocchio*, Chapter 4.

The story is trying to provide a moral lesson about the foolishness of vagabond youth, but all I could notice is what a poor job the Talking Cricket does at explaining why one has to work. The Cricket is described as being patient and philosophical, and promises to tell Pinocchio a "great truth" ... but then just gives the vague warning of "woe to boys who rebel—they never come to any good." The Cricket *begins* to give a valid explanation when he suggests that Pinocchio learn a trade, yet he doesn't follow through with reasons that Pinocchio can understand: the Cricket's words have to be taken on faith alone. Pinocchio's stance, on the other hand, is at least based on his real-life experience. And based on his limited and sheltered experience of "being a vagabond = fun" and "work and school = not fun," his stance makes perfect sense! What Pinocchio needed was for the Talking Cricket to explain, without overtones of haughtiness, the specific drawback behind a sole focus on immediate pleasure: the lack of a reliable food supply when you haven't yet learned the skills to hunt or grow or trade for it. Pinocchio needed the Talking Cricket to patiently explain why "eating, drinking, sleeping, and amusing oneself" cannot be considered a trade. (*What* is he "trading," and with whom?)

It may be that Pinocchio had to learn the hard way. Maybe he could learn only by experiencing such a ravenous gnawing in his stomach that he ends up scavenging for bones discarded by dogs and for moldy pudding left in trashcans, all the while repeating his cry, "Oh! What a dreadful illness hunger is!" Certainly it makes for a better story. But in real life, self-interest dictates that we try our best to avoid unnecessary misery. And Pinocchio's period of starvation and the Talking Cricket's death (as well as other violent conflicts in Pinocchio's life) could have had a better chance of being avoided had Pinocchio received an explanation that had empathy for a person new to the world. An explanation that went beyond "be a good boy because I said so."

# 2. Surgery & Dental Floss: the complications of bartering

Back in the hunting and gathering days there was no need for money. And when people first began to specialize in raising crops and making tools, those few products were probably just directly traded for each other—still no need for money. But advances in agriculture meant less people were needed to produce the community's food: this in turn meant more people were free to develop specialized skills, which in turn greatly complicated the bartering process.

Let's use ancient Egypt as an example. As far back as 2500 B.C., its cities were full of farmers, tailors, architects, pottery sculptors, papyrus-processors (the processed papyrus plant was used as paper), etc. Now suppose an ancient Egyptian architect needed some writing paper. There might be several papyrus-processors to choose from, but suppose none of them had any use for an architect? Or suppose a papyrus-processor wanted some olives, but none of the local olive growers had any use for paper? Suppose an olive grower needed an architect, but couldn't find one who liked olives?

This shows one of the drawbacks of an economic system based on barter: you can't trade with someone who doesn't want what you've got. Accordingly, you have to spend lots of time and energy finding people whose needs are precisely complementary with yours. Economists call this the *double coincidence of wants* problem, and note that solving this problem requires multi-good communities to find some sort of object that will serve as a *medium-of-exchange*, a *measure-of-value*, and a *store-of-value*.

## A Medium-of-Exchange

If everyone in a community can agree to use a certain object (be it shells, beads, or dollar bills) as a *medium-of-exchange* (that is, an object, or "medium" for trading), the *double coincidence of wants* problem is solved. Unlike specific goods and services, an agreed-upon medium-of-exchange will almost always be of value to *everyone* in the community, because that medium-of-exchange can be used to trade for every product and every service the community has. If the above Egyptian architect, olive grower, and papyrus-processor all used a medium-of-exchange of say, silver, their bartering problems would disappear: the architect could use silver to trade for the papyrus, the papyrus-processor would be happy to accept the silver because he could trade it for olives, and the olive grower would gladly accept the silver because he could use it to trade for services from the architect.

As important as using some form of currency became during the First Wave, it became all the more necessary as the number of goods increased during the Second and Third Waves. Imagine a modern industry such as movie-making using the bartering system: movie lines filled with people holding goods and promising services, with the filmmakers and crew wading through the crowd to see what they were interested in—for every showing at every location! It's thanks to the use of a medium-of-exchange that a wide variety of people—whether pottery sculptors or videogame programmers—can all go to any movie they want, regardless of the link between their specialized skills and the filmmaker's personal interests. Whether a filmmaker has any interest in pottery or videogames doesn't matter, because the use of a medium-of-exchange allows for the trade to operate independently of the filmmaker's desires for his audience's particular goods and services. And in turn, the medium-of-exchange collected by the filmmaker can then be used to trade for any product or service he might want—even surgery from a physician who's not a movie-goer.

## A Measure-of-Value

Suppose two or more traders in a bartering community just happen to hit upon that elusive *double coincidence of wants*. Suppose during the course of an unusual day, a carpenter who needs a winter coat and knee surgery and some dental floss just happens to come in contact with a tailor and a surgeon and a floss-maker—all of whom need tables. The *double coincidence of wants* problem may not be an issue, but the carpenter still faces the difficulty of determining what price—or more accurately, what price*s*—to charge for his tables. For the tailor it might be an even trade for the coat, but for the floss-maker the price might be fifty rolls … and for the surgeon, the table may count as only one-tenth of the trade for the operation. Barter with the floss-maker would leave our carpenter with more floss than he probably wants,[i] and the barter for surgery might not go through unless the surgeon was interested in acquiring a whole dining set.

This shows another problem with bartering: it results in multiple prices for each good and service, which in turn results in complicated negotiations and massive record keeping. The above carpenter has enough headaches with the price of a single table, let alone the rest of his inventory. At first glance, bartering seems simpler and somehow more "honest" than using money, but the logistical problems are a nightmare. With bartering, every good and service in society must be quoted in terms of every other good and service. If a bartering community had only 100 goods, each good would need 99 prices of its own, adding up to a total of 9,900 prices! But when an agreed-upon common denominator of money is used as a measuring tool (that is, a *measure-of-value*), each good needs only one price. By switching from a bartering to a monetary system, a community with 100 goods goes from having nearly 10,000 prices to only 100.

. . .

Feeling estranged from the rapidly industrializing world around him, the American philosopher Henry David Thoreau (1817–1862) moved to an isolated cabin in the woods so he could, as described in his book *Walden*, "live deliberately, to front only the essential facts of life, and see if I could not learn what it had to teach …" Reducing dependency on money by building his own shelter and growing his own food was part of

---

[i] Plus, this creates another *double coincidence of wants* problem: because the carpenter would be so over-stocked with floss, the floss-maker couldn't hope to make any future trades with him for several years.

Thoreau's life-simplifying mission, but he also writes of a conversation that taught him why using money was in fact simpler than barter:

> When I asked him [the woodchopper] if he could do without money, he showed the convenience of money in such a way as to suggest the most philosophical accounts of the origin of this institution ... If an ox were his property, and he wished to get needles and thread at the store, he thought it would be inconvenient and impossible to go on mortgaging some portion of the creature each time to that amount.[ii]

. . .

## A Store-of-Value

One of the challenges a community must meet in agreeing upon a medium-of-exchange and measure-of-value is finding something that will store well for future use, that's easy to divide, easy to transport, and is sufficiently rare. Many different forms were tried in the past, and most ended up being replaced due to various problems: wheat goes bad over time, salt dissolves in the rain, cattle doesn't divide conveniently, and objects like sticks and rocks would never work because they're not rare—people would never be willing to exchange their goods and services for a medium-of-exchange they could just find anywhere on their own. Gold and silver met the requirements for storage, division, transportation, and rareness better than most forms, and ended up being a widely accepted medium. One problem these metals *did* have was the hassle of having to weigh them before every transaction. To solve this, governments came to put official stamps on measured pieces of gold and silver to mark their value—thus the creation of coins. A remaining problem was the coins' heavy weight (if you had enough of them). Again as a matter of convenience and efficiency, government-issued paper money gradually came to serve as an alternative.[6]

The newer form of money as a purely electronic account is the most convenient and efficient store-of-value yet. This is a medium in which

---

[ii] Henry David Thoreau, *Walden and Other Writings*. Quotes from pp. 172 and 215.

trillions of dollars can be stored using hardly any space at all, division is painless, spoilage and tarnishing are of no concern, and transportation—even over thousands of miles—is instantaneous and practically effortless. Electronic currency does seem, however, to violate the necessary quality of being "rare." In a way, it seems even more plentiful than sticks and rocks. When I took an economics course, I asked the professor if he thought this medium-of-exchange was trustworthy: isn't it too easy for unscrupulous computer hackers to simply create millions of dollars? Why do I labor hard at work just to be rewarded with something so "unrare"—something so easy to type in, and so easy to backspace over? His reply was that the supply of electronic money is *not* unlimited, but tightly controlled by the Federal Reserve System. He added that while it's true that electronic accounts raise new types of security issues, counterfeiting is an ancient art, and no form of money has ever been absolutely foolproof. His position was that the controls over electronic currency are actually superior to the controls over coins and paper bills: records are now more accurate, more reliable, and replacement issues and other problems are more easily resolved. He said that despite whatever mistrust one may feel toward a medium-of-exchange that's void of substance, electronic currency *does* work, and often much better than conventional forms. I had to admit that I've found this to be true ... using a debit card at supermarkets is more convenient than having to carry cash, electronic bill payments don't get lost in the mail or need stamps, and using an E-Z Pass for highway tolls is a breeze compared to waiting in long tollbooth lines.

. . .

The above definitions show that the form of money a community agrees upon—whether beads or bills or electrons—is generally worth something only within the confines of that community. In the movie *The Gods Must Be Crazy II,* a wealthy businesswoman traveling in Africa misses this point and attempts to use American dollars to win favors from a Bushman, who just looks at her with puzzled amusement. Similarly frustrated with the worthlessness of his money is the island-marooned Robinson Crusoe, who moans that the "treasure" of gold he finds on a wrecked ship wouldn't be worth the effort of stooping down to pick it up, and cries, "O drug! ... what art thou good for?"[iii] And Voltaire's character Candide is bewildered when he finds he's in a country where gold, due to the local abundance, is considered valueless:

> When the meal was over, Cacambo and Candide thought they had amply paid their bill when they left on the table two of the big pieces of gold they had picked up, but the host and hostess burst out laughing and held their sides for a long time.
> "Gentlemen," said the host, "it's easy to see you're not from our country, and we're not used to foreigners. Excuse us for laughing when you offered to pay us with two stones from our roads."[iv]

The dismay of Crusoe, Candide, and the businesswoman over the uselessness of their money suggests the foolishness of their (and society's) obsession with something as trite as paper bills and yellow rocks. But the only foolishness is the characters' beliefs that the value of their money is somehow within itself, rather than the value coming from their home community's agreement to use it as a medium for trading. (This is why the U.S. government, back in 1971, could abandon the "gold standard"—the promise that currency holders could convert their bills into gold. The main thing that makes gold valuable is our community's agreement to use it as a medium-of-exchange: the switch to a system based on government-printed paper money was just a switch to a medium that's easier to create.)

. . .

I like to think of money as something that permits flexible bartering. Thanks to the use of money, I can wait tables for eight hours one night, store that labor in my pocket (via cash), and the next morning barter it for all the labor behind the making of a pair of shoes, a box of light bulbs, a bicycle lock, and a gallon of milk. Without a medium-of-

---

[iii] Daniel Defoe, *Robinson Crusoe* (p. 47 in Penguin Putnam's 2001 edition).

[iv] Francois Voltaire, *Candide*, Chapter 17 (p. 65 in Bantam Books' 1984 edition).

exchange, this sort of wonderfully flexible trading would be impossible. This convenience, however, does come at a price.

The dictionary defines *alienation* as "a withdrawing of a person's affections from an object of former attachment." This well-describes what happens when we labor for a medium-of-exchange, rather than for something tangible such as growing our food or building our homes (as will be discussed further in Chapter 4, *Emperors & Emptiness*). When the efforts of our labor are translated into money, the end reward just doesn't seem quite as precious. It's kind of like what happens when a poem from one of the romance languages is translated into English: something gets lost along the way.

The alienating aspect of a medium-of-exchange allows us to be oblivious to the fact that what we're really still doing is trading, albeit indirectly. When people have financial problems, they'll sometimes mistakenly identify money itself as the enemy. An example of this kind of error can be seen in the following excerpt from a letter from the penniless Vincent Van Gogh to his brother Theo:

> If you lived in times of war, you might possibly have to fight, you would regret it, you would lament that you weren't living in times of peace, but after all the necessity would be there and you would fight.
>
> And in the same way we certainly have the right to wish for a state of things in which money would not be necessary in order to live. However, as everything is done by money now, one has got to think about making it so long as one spends it ...[v]

But if Van Gogh's hometown didn't use money, its members would still have to labor for their food, clothing and shelter. The absence of money doesn't mean survival basics appear spontaneously. In fact, the use of money *increases* opportunities for those such as Van Gogh to survive via their artistic gifts, because using a medium-of-exchange broadens the number of potential traders by eliminating the *double coincidence of wants* problem. If Van Gogh's community ran on barter, his base of potential customers would have shrunk to only those such as farmers,

---

[v] Vincent Van Gogh, *The Letters of Vincent Van Gogh*, p. 293.

shelter-builders, and paint and canvas suppliers—shrunk to that limited number of laborers who could offer products that Van Gogh could use in return. Van Gogh's poverty did not stem from his community's use of money, but from his inability to find *anyone* who wanted his artwork: whether canvas makers, ship builders, diamond miners, or fashion designers. (That is, of course, during his lifetime—today his paintings sell for millions.) The alienating quality of money lends itself to this kind of misplaced blame.

This alienation worsens as the increasingly convenient forms we use for money become increasingly abstract. Paper money doesn't seem as "real" as precious metals such as gold and silver, and electronic money barely seems to exist at all. My knowledge of the Federal Reserve System's controls over electronic currency notwithstanding, I'll still sometimes stare at the numbers on my bank statement and wonder how they represent any real value. After all, anybody can type numbers on a piece of paper. I know the numbers that *I* type are worthless, whereas the bank's numbers are somehow officially "approved" and good for trade … but it's still an abstract difference. It doesn't seem as real as the difference between barren soil and a field full of crops (although it *is* the modern equivalent). An example of a common negative consequence of this alienation is the way so many people postpone building retirement accounts. If you tell me I need to work hard in the spring, summer, and fall in order to stock up on grain and dried fruit so I won't starve in the winter—that's direct and motivating. If you tell me I need to stock up on electronic numbers so I won't starve when I'm too old to work … well, that's abstract and a bit easier to ignore.

Understanding the pros and cons of using a medium-of-exchange helps us to come to peace with having to use it. Paper bills and electronic accounts may be alienating, but we should also recognize that they do great jobs at (1) solving the *double coincidence of wants* problem, (2) serving as a measure-of-value, and (3) being a convenient store-of-value (try to picture storing grain for your retirement). In my early twenties I listened to co-workers' theories about how this country needed a revolution to abolish money, and how this move would somehow improve life. But if such a revolution were unfortunate enough to succeed, its leaders would soon be left scratching their heads saying,

"Well ... I guess we didn't think this all the way through ..." once confronted with the inevitable frustration of the public—farmers who found it impossible to schedule trading sessions with all their customers, and teachers overwhelmed with the logistics of bartering with hundreds of students every semester. And imagine the nightmare of a barter system trying to run public transportation![7]

# 3. Penguins & Peacocks: Darwin's "direction"

Some look at the evolution of our workday and describe it as progress, noting that the accumulated knowledge that resulted from specialization is what led the human race to achieve our triumphs in art, science, medicine, and engineering. Those who long for the simpler and supposedly more peaceful past look at the same history and bemoan our road toward ruin: ozone depletion, wildlife destruction, tabloid journalism, etc. Each side can sound convincing when presenting its selective evidence. Looking at the larger picture, however, I believe we can see a more accurate view of our "direction"—one that has a parallel to evolution in nature.

A common theme in scientist Stephen Jay Gould's essays is how people often misunderstand Darwin's theory of evolution, associating the word *evolution* with the implications in the word *evolved*, as if evolution were necessarily about improvement. Through a close examination of our surroundings—such as flies and beetles that devour their mothers from the inside, and the panda's "thumb" (really a bone sticking out of its wrist)—Gould argues that our quirky world of imperfections and odd solutions offer strong evidence that nature's only concerns are reproductive success and survival within the local environment.[i] Rather than being a breeder with long-term goals in mind, nature simply favors the organisms that are the most successful at passing on their genes to future generations. The evolution of our workday follows the same "direction," or lack of. The hunting and gathering lifestyle has largely disappeared simply because the agricultural lifestyle does a better job at passing on genes to future generations. Likewise, those who adopted industry had better "reproductive success" than did those who stuck only to agriculture or hunting and gathering—especially when these different groups met in conflict (see details in endnotes 2–4).

---

[i] The fly in mention is the cecidomyian gall midge, the beetle is the micromalthus debilis (see pp. 91–92 in Gould's *Ever Since Darwin*), and Gould's essay "The Panda's Thumb" is the first chapter in his book by the same name.

Adaptive changes sometimes *do* benefit the long-term interests of a species. For example, penguins that happen to be born with oilier feathers than their siblings are faster swimmers (the oil waterproofs their feathers and cuts back on water resistance), so they're more likely to escape attacks from predators, and thus more likely to reproduce than their slower siblings. And because many traits are passed down by heredity, the offspring of these oily-feathered penguins are also likely to have oily feathers: consequently, this trait starts to spread to the species as a whole. This particular adaptation benefits penguins' short-term circumstances as well as their long-term interests, but evolution doesn't always work out that way. Sometimes adaptive changes that enhance success in the short-term will actually weaken success in the long-term. For example, the longer and more striking a peacock's tail feathers are, the more females he'll attract. These Casanovas will pass on the most genes to future generations, but this adaptation works against the species' long-term survival prospects (at least out in the wild): their beautiful but clumsy tails make it more difficult to escape from predators.

Like the feathers of the peacock, human developments that best support our short-term interests will sometimes sabotage our prospects for long-term survival. Nuclear weaponry, its creation justified for survival during World War II (in that Nazi Germany was working on an atomic bomb of its own), is the best example of this. And like the feathers of the penguin, changes driven by short-term circumstances sometimes *do* parallel our long-term interests, such as habit changes brought on by our increased knowledge about exercise and nutrition. Still, the immediate benefits are what drives most of human behavior … for example, it's not necessarily contradictory for a person to follow an aerobic workout with a visit to a tanning booth: one activity helps to increase longevity (by keeping the heart strong) and the other threatens to cut it short (by increasing the risk of skin cancer), but both have direct payoffs.

Unlike peacocks, of course, humans can make predictions about how our short-term practices will affect our long-term interests. Unlike all other animals, we can do things to protect our future, such as passing laws on safety standards for clean air, clean water, and ultraviolet emissions. But my intention here is not to preach about the environment or use of sunscreen; my only aim is to try to make sense out of something that often seems *not* to make sense. For those who focus primarily on the negative aspects of modern life and ask "Why did we do this to ourselves?", I'm just saying that it's easier to understand the world when we realize that change will always be predominately driven by the immediate demands of survival and reproductive success, not by long-range optimality.

# PART II: WORK, WEALTH, & HAPPINESS

# 4. Emperors & Emptiness

The poet Lanza Del Vasto wrote that one of the paths to a more peaceful life was to "find the shortest, simplest way between the earth, the hands, and the mouth." Today we have a long, complicated way between the earth, hands, and mouth. We eat fruits and vegetables without ever touching the soil, and eat chicken and beef without ever even seeing, much less killing, the animals we consume. We also never see the long line of people who handle our food before it reaches us: those who raise the meat and produce first-hand, those who package it, those who ship it, etc. And our "trade" for this food—the goods and services from our own professions—usually involves a similarly circuitous path. But does this complexity really give us any day-to-day problems?

After all, our complicated system comes with lots of benefits. The most immediate advantage is that we're no longer directly dependent on the pitiless elements. We can scarcely imagine what it was like back in the days when droughts and bitter winters meant increased hunger and death: harsh weather conditions today, at least for most of us, rarely cause more than inconveniences. The average modern American is not only free from periodic threats of starvation, but in many ways lives with even greater luxuries than those of yesteryear's royalty. Thanks to specialization, the results of our workday include heat in the winter, air conditioning in the summer, hot and cold water whenever we want it, a wide variety of food from all over the world during every season, refrigerators and freezers for food storage, medicine to cure and prevent formerly crippling and life-threatening diseases, and technology that gives us access to instant communication around the world as well as staggering amounts of stored knowledge and 24-hour-a-day entertainment. What's the problem?

Back in the mid-1800s, Karl Marx wrote that one of the problems with this new industrial system was that the modern worker ended up suffering from alienation, as labor was being divided in such a way that workers no longer created and owned the final product, or even owned the tools of their craft. Marx argued that this lack of creation and ownership gave the laborer a sense of purposelessness. The carpenter who makes a table has a sense of pride with the end result, but the factory worker who performs only a monotonous task for hours on end has nothing tangible at the close of the day, nothing but a paycheck (as discussed in Chapter 2, regarding the results of our labor being translated into a medium-of-exchange). Back once again to Adam Smith's pin factory story: the new division of labor meant an individual worker's output went from 20 pins per day to over 4,800, but it also meant a change from a system where workers knew how to make a complete product, to a system where workers didn't know how to do anything except perform one repetitive movement. The product may have become more marketable, but workers' skills were destroyed along the way. Farmer and author Wendell Berry writes that this "disease of specialization" leaves us divorced from personal wholeness, in the sense that we no longer know how to provide ourselves with survival basics independently. He claims the result is a feeling of helplessness, since "a specialist ... can do virtually nothing for himself" and relies on other specialists for everything from food and water to education and entertainment.[i]

Another social critic, Paul Goodman, wrote the following about the damaging effects of alienation in his 1956 book *Growing Up Absurd:*

> It's hard to grow up when there isn't enough man's work. There is "nearly full employment" ... but there get to be fewer jobs that are necessary or unquestionably useful ... To produce necessary food and shelter is man's work. During most of economic history most men have done this drudging work, secure that it was justified and worthy ... Once we turn away from the absolutely necessary subsistence jobs, however, we find that an enormous proportion of our production is not even unquestionably useful.[8] ... If there is nothing worthwhile, it

---

[i] Wendell Berry, *The Unsettling of America: Culture & Agriculture*, p. 21. Berry continues: "In living in the world by his own will and skill, the stupidest peasant or tribesman is more competent than the most intelligent worker or technician or intellectual in a society of specialists."

is hard to do anything at all. When one does nothing, one is threatened by the question, *is* one nothing?[ii]

Thoreau, in *Life without Principle*, goes so far as to say:

Cold and hunger seem more friendly to my nature than those methods which men have adopted and advise to ward them off.[iii]

Another drawback of today's system comes from the way our expectations shift when we're immersed in a society overflowing with goods and services. Given that there's so much to desire, there's also that much more of a margin for feeling deprived when we see others who have more than we do. In his book *Luxury Fever*, economist Robert Frank points out that making extra money doesn't necessarily alleviate this feeling of deprivation—for the only reliable correlation between an increase in wealth and an increase in happiness occurs when people rise from below the poverty line to above it. Once above that line, people's standards simply rise along with their economic gains, leaving a zero gain in happiness.[9]

Our wide range of work options is another blessing that comes with drawbacks. Though it seems as if it should be a purely liberating experience to be free from the old tradition of inheriting a parent's occupation, having an abundance of career opportunities also gives us an abundance of opportunities for failure. This problem is aggravated by the way we link our employment to our very identity. We're less likely to worry about bare survival the way our ancestors did, but this opens up the luxury to be stressed about a host of psychological problems. It may be no accident that the field of psychiatry arose shortly after the Industrial Revolution—the Revolution increased the number of things to be neurotic about.

---

[ii] Paul Goodman, *Growing Up Absurd*, pp. 17, 18, 41.

[iii] Henry David Thoreau, *Walden and Other Writings*, p. 360 (... although I can't help but feel that if Thoreau were truly freezing and starving, exchanging data-entry labor for a wool blanket and a warm loaf of bread would start to look damn attractive).

For most of us, the advantages of today's specialist-saturated world go a long way in making up for the disadvantages. Personally, I'll gladly accept the manageable risks of neurosis and alienation in exchange for the benefits of polio vaccinations and indoor plumbing. On the other hand, I also agree with the social critics who charge that the modern guideline for our workday—the never-ending pursuit of more status, more wealth, and more possessions—is an unreliable route to having a happy life. The next two chapters discuss alternatives to the materialistic approach to life that unquestioningly accepts our culture's guideline, as well as alternatives to the rebellious (and usually broke and dependent) approach that unquestioningly rejects it.[10]

# 5. *More* vs. *Enough*

Back in the Cro-Magnon days it was easier to recognize when we had "enough." After a cave-family had their basics for survival covered, what else did they need? Today there's a limitless sea of products to "need"— a sea that gets only wider and deeper as technology continues to advance. Furthermore, many of the purchases we make are unrelated to our desire for the product itself, but are made for reasons such as displaying status, attempting to gain or prove love, or just alleviating boredom. The commercials that continually bombard us perpetuate our spending by trying to convince us that there are holes in our lives, holes that can be filled only upon buying the advertised product.

Combine (a) our enormous number of goods and services with (b) the excessive number of reasons we have for spending and (c) an electronic currency that's both alienating and practically effortless to exchange, and you have the recipe for overspending. Overcharging on credit cards is probably the best example of how an alienating and overly convenient medium-of-exchange contributes to spending more than we can afford. Would we be as likely to overcharge if we were trading with the physical products of our labor? If we had spent long hours crafting a table, would we be as likely to make spur-of-the-moment exchanges for it? Just as our efficient food distribution system tempts us to eat beyond satisfying our physical needs, our efficient monetary system tempts us to spend beyond our material needs.

In the book *Your Money or Your Life*, authors Joe Dominguez and Vicki Robin offer a solution to this problem through a method they call "conscious spending." First, they ask you to think of money as "something we choose to trade our life energy for," and then to examine how much enjoyment you've gotten from your purchases relative to the number of life hours you traded for them. We may not have a strong emotional attachment to numbers promised to a credit card, but our life hours are real—tangible and finite. This approach, in other words, tries to reduce the alienating aspect of our medium-of-exchange by translating our dollars into something that *is* precious: our time.[11] Take a $59.95 yearly subscription to a magazine rarely read. If your "real hourly wage"[i] is $10.00 an hour, then you're trading that subscription for six hours of your labor. Based on the amount of enjoyment you receive from the magazines relative to the number of hours you had to work for their purchase, you may decide that this is not the kind of trade you want to continue.

Dominguez and Robin recommend that you measure all your purchases against the time it took you to earn the money spent on those purchases. Armed with this knowledge, you can then reevaluate your spending and reconsider expenses that don't contribute to your needs or happiness: recreational shopping, excessive restaurant dining and take-outs, toys that will hold a child's interest for no more than ten minutes, buying books that could have been borrowed from the library, purchases made for the sole purpose of trying to impress others, and so on. Conscious spending is compared to a diet that doesn't count calories or measure portions, but just sticks to the following rules: (1) eat only when you're hungry, (2) pay close attention to when you're no longer hungry, and (3) stop.

Why dedicate all this attention to tracking income and expenses? The answer depends on whether you live dependently or independently. If you can rely on your parents or whomever for food, clothing and shelter, then maybe the only drawback of overspending is an inability to buy any more non-necessities until more money comes your way. Overspending isn't always a problem if you're a dependent ... but it *is* a dangerous habit, because it leads to all sorts of concrete miseries once you're independent. Shut-off utilities, eviction notices, and untreated cavities are a few that come to mind. Switching from a "more is better" to a "conscious spending" mindset means you gain greater control over your life: money previously spent on things that don't matter becomes available for things that do.

---

[i] Dominguez and Robin make a distinction between the hourly wage you see on your paycheck, and what they call your "real hourly wage," which is calculated by (1) adding the value of your job's benefits, (2) deducting *all* your work-related expenses, and (3) dividing your remaining pay by *all* the hours your job consumes. Details in endnote 11.

So if *more* money isn't better, yet *some* is vital, how much is *enough*? Financial advice books generally recommend variations on the following:

## The Four Levels of Enough

Level 1
Enough to cover all types of daily, monthly, and yearly expenses:
(a) a budget for predictable expenses: food, clothing, rent, phone, electricity, car insurance, birthday and holiday gifts, etc.
(b) a budget for irregular expenses: repairs, replacements, out-of-pocket medical bills, etc. (A monthly budget for such expenses can be set by estimating their yearly costs, and then dividing that figure by twelve.)

Level 2
Enough beyond Level 1 to pay off your debts: credit cards, college loans, etc.

Level 3
Enough to build a reserve fund equal to about six months of living expenses.

Level 4
Enough beyond Level 3 to be able to invest for large future expenses, the two most common being retirement and a child's college tuition.

Ideally, these four levels should be achieved in order. For example, you probably shouldn't start building Level 3's reserve cushion (generally held in a safe but low-yield account) until you have Level 2's debts paid off. Putting Level 3 before Level 2 could mean gaining as low as 1% interest while paying as high as 20%. Similarly, it's recommended that you shouldn't start Level 4's long-term investment plans before building Level 3's reserve cushion. Long-term investments usually include stocks, and stocks are not about immediate moneymaking: the market fluctuates, and the high interest is generally gained only over a period of years.

Investments should not be counted upon in times of emergency—such a use can result in taking a financial loss. That's why a backup supply equal to about six months worth of living expenses should be built up first, and stored in a no-risk place such as a savings account.[ii]

Our ability to invest money for Level 4 is made more difficult by the belief that the few dollars we carelessly spend here and there don't matter. But suppose we took, say, the extra $5 per day that goes toward buying lunch Monday through Friday rather than bringing it from home, and invested that money instead. If your investments from that $5 per workday (that is, $25/week, $100/month, $1,200/year) yielded an annual average of 8.4%,[iii] in ten years it would build to $18,709, in twenty years to $61, 918, and in forty years to $392,202! Small amounts *do* add up.

This shows what a difference the element of time makes, as time allows interest to generate interest upon itself, or to *compound*. For those unfamiliar with compounding, let's say you make a one-time investment of $1,000. In the first year, say it earns 10%, or $100. Now your total is $1,100. During the second year, your interest—that extra $100—will also be generating interest. If you earn 10% again, the interest on your $1,100 will come to $110. Now you've got a total of $1,210 working for you, and so on.

The best way to take advantage of compounding is to start investing when we're young, which unfortunately is when we're least capable, not to mention the least interested. Despite these figures, I don't know if I could convince a 20-year-old version of myself to start investing. Maybe this is because I found electronic accounts alienating, or maybe because I didn't think I'd ever get old. Whatever the reason, investing just didn't

---

[ii] There are exceptions. For example, many employers offer 401K retirement plans (a Level 4 concern) in which the company matches a percentage of your contribution. In effect this is a raise that, in most cases, should not be turned down, even if you're still struggling with Levels 1, 2, and 3.

[iii] 8.4% is the average growth rate for the S&P 500 between 1950 and 2001. Source: David Edwards, "Charting Your Way to Stock Gains," from www.TheStreet.com, 7 March 2002. (S&P 500 = a collection of 500 stocks that are considered to be widely held, and representative of the stock market as a whole. I'll add the typical disclaimer that goes with all mention of stocks and interest: "Past performance is not necessarily indicative of future results.")

seem relevant to me until my thirties. But for those who *can* get over obstacles such as alienation and illusions of eternal youth, consider how much it takes to have a million dollars by the time you reach age sixty-five. To again assume an annual average of 8.4% interest, you would have to invest $985 per month if you began when you were forty, $395 per month if you began when you were thirty, and only $166 per month if you began when you were twenty.

The thought of studying up on investments, debt management, stocks and mutual funds, etc. may seem dreary, but working excess hours—and excess *years*—can be dreary too! Wise use of your money can decrease the time you have to spend at your job: it's worth the investment of time it takes either to get professional advice, or at least to read a few financial self-help books.

Reaching a monthly income that will satisfy Levels 1–4 will vary wildly from person to person: a writer whose needs are limited to a computer and access to a library will need considerably less money than a paleontologist whose needs include financing archeological digs. It will be more difficult for some than for others to reach this definition of *enough*, but at least this guideline has a concrete goal. At least it has a chance of being attained, unlike the impossible-by-definition goal of "making more than I make now." And if these four levels *can* be reached and maintained, *enough* has been achieved—increasing your income no longer need be a dominating or compromising concern.[12]

Now, by no means does the achievement of these four levels guarantee happiness. You can have Levels 1–4 and far beyond, and still have plenty of room in your life for misery due to poor health, unsatisfying personal relationships, or the random tragedies that life sometimes distributes. Having *enough* money, however, does eliminate a significant amount of money-related stress. Below Level 1, affording even basics such as phone service becomes a struggle. Below Level 3, a large setback such as losing your job can bring on great hardships; below Level 4, you may end up having insufficient money in the future for independent survival.

Rather than equating any level of money with achieving happiness itself, I think of having sufficient money as being a *foundation* for happiness. A foundation alone won't provide shelter, but it will provide sturdiness should you build a home upon it. Materialistic people fixated on wealth will ignore building that home and just create a massive foundation, and may later be surprised to find that it won't keep them dry and warm. Rebels who believe that money doesn't matter will ignore the foundation, and may later be surprised to find their homes falling apart.

# 6. Measuring Success

In his book *Working,* Studs Terkel writes that "[Work is] a search … for daily meaning as well as daily bread, for recognition as well as cash …"[i] He also writes that our workday often includes violence to the spirit as well as the body. This "violence to the spirit" is what happens when our expectations of finding meaning and recognition go unmet.

Intensified since the Industrial Revolution, we look to our jobs for our source of personal growth, our sense of importance, and our very identities. Phrases such as "I *am* a graphic designer" are part of our language rather than "I *do* graphic designing." And judging from the media, as well as from parents who want their children to be "doctors or lawyers," the typical measure of a job's success is the wealth and status it brings. But is using our employment as our route to our identity and fulfillment a reliable guideline for having a happy life?

Looking at the positive aspects of today's work system, it admittedly does give us many more chances for fulfillment than it used to. As opposed to earlier days when most people had no choice but to spend their whole lives doing physical labor, there are now options to earn our food, clothing and shelter by use of our skills and talents: in art, athletics, education, medical care, etc. And given that our jobs usually take up forty or more hours a week of our time, it does make sense to strive for a job we find enjoyable in some way. A significant border around our career decision, however, is that our jobs must provide a good or service that other people are willing to trade with.

Suppose someone's gift is creating paintings that, like Van Gogh's, nobody wants to buy? Or even if such artists *can* succeed in attracting buyers, suppose combining one's art with one's income means being in an environment where the competition is so cutthroat that all the joy is lost? The idea that our route to recognition *must* come through our paid employment rests on the premise that our most treasured talents will have a place in the competitive and sometimes overcrowded market: a

---

[i] Studs Terkel, *Working*, p. xi.

premise that for many isn't true. For such people, the results of internally accepting the Paid Employment = Identity premise will be high stress or poverty (and often both) if they stick solely to what they feel is their true calling, or frustration as they work other jobs to pay their bills. Depression is another possible result, especially if a talent is altogether abandoned just because it doesn't serve well as a vehicle for trade.

It's true that we need paid employment in order to satisfy our physical needs for food, clothing and shelter, but as thinkers throughout the ages have pointed out, "the physical" is only one component of life. The ancient Indian *Rig Veda*, for example, says our lives are made up of three components: Body, Mind, and Soul. The Greek philosopher Plato also refers to three parts of man, calling them Appetite, Reason, and Spirit. Recent philosophers speak of four components, having divided the "Mind" aspect into two—one for "emotional," the other for "knowledge." Author Stephen Covey calls these our "Four Dimensions," describing them as the Physical, the Social/Emotional, the Mental, and the Spiritual. Aldous Huxley expresses a similar division, using the terms Body, Character, Abstract Knowledge, and Soul. Writer and running guru George Sheehan, along the same lines, stresses the importance of our "four roles": being a good Animal, Friend, Craftsman, and Saint. Suppose our pursuit of happiness was sought through achieving a satisfactory balance of these Four Dimensions, rather than through the wealth and status that comes from our careers? Here's what I mean in chart form:

# The Four Dimensions Map[ii]

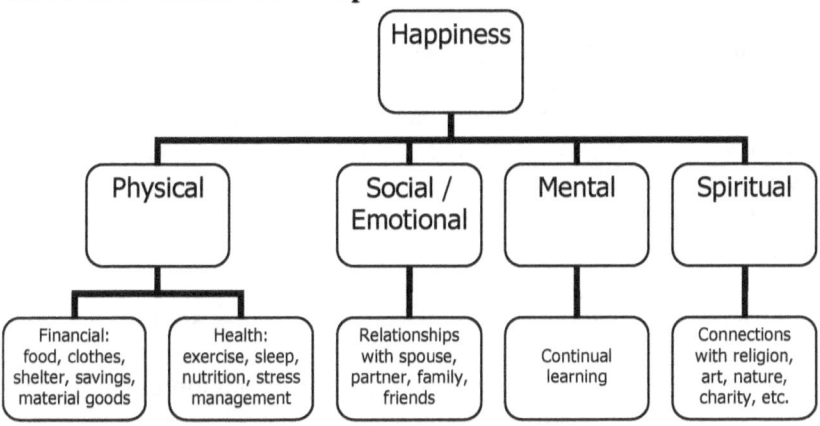

Contrast this with our culture's more typical measure of success:

# The Wealth & Status Map

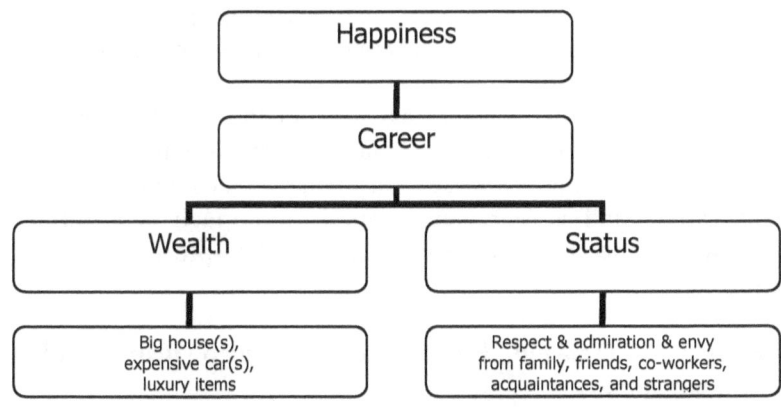

---

[ii] This chart should not be interpreted to mean that everyone should give each dimension an equal 25%, or give that attention in any set way. Satisfaction in the Social/Emotional dimension, for example, may center around a spouse and children for some, and for others it may entail a large network of friends. One person may categorize yoga as a physical exercise; another person may categorize it as a spiritual exercise. The chart's only assumption is that these four broad categories are all important aspects of happiness: the way they are fulfilled is individually defined.

I admit that the focus on success as measured by wealth and status has brought us many great goods and services—I fully appreciate being in a world with well-stocked grocery shelves and anesthesia during surgery. But because the pursuit of wealth and status fulfills only limited aspects of our physical and social dimensions, and tends to neglect all else, I believe it's an unreliable guideline for achieving personal happiness. Below is a look at the shortcomings of the Wealth & Status mindset in respect to our Physical, Social/Emotional, Mental, and Spiritual dimensions:

### The Physical Dimension, Financial (food, clothing, shelter, savings, material goods)

The Wealth & Status map generally does an adequate job at taking care of our basic financial needs. (As the saying goes, "I've been poor and I've been rich, and believe me, rich is better.") The problem is that it doesn't stop with providing us with *enough*. Rather, "more is better" is the Wealth & Status map's measuring tool for our job title, living quarters, and material belongings. Accordingly, "whatever I've got now" can *never* be enough, as *more* is an ever-receding horizon: a guideline that always leaves us subject to disappointment when we see someone else's material display outdo our own.

An excessive focus on acquiring *more* in fact threatens having the type of material wealth that *does* matter, such as having a budgeted amount for irregular expenses, a reserve cushion in case of unemployment, and a retirement plan. If too much is spent on the outward appearance of wealth, important but low-profile funds end up jeopardized.

### The Physical Dimension, Health (exercise, sleep, proper nutrition, stress management)

This subsection of the Physical dimension has no role in the Wealth & Status map. A person may be exhausted, ulcer-ridden, and on the verge of a heart attack—but if business is good, she or he still earns the broad title of being a "success."

**The Emotional / Social Dimension (relationships with others)**
The Wealth & Status map's attention to the social dimension comes through pursuing career goals that will win the admiration and envy of family, friends, co-workers, acquaintances, and strangers. Now, having a career that others admire doesn't necessarily run contrary to personal fulfillment. But if "impressiveness" is the primary reason that a particular career is chosen, how likely is it to be internally satisfying if that satisfaction has to come from the opinions of others? And besides, does one-upping those around you actually bring about genuine admiration? It might work sometimes … but it also generates jealousy, resentment, and false friends.

In *Power! How to Get It, How to Use It*—a book that mainly extols power's benefits—author Michael Korda does admit that attaining positions of power comes with the drawback of creating a distance between formerly close relationships. Korda acknowledges, as a sidenote, that "somehow the path of power is seldom the path of love." One interviewee, the owner of a world-famous magazine, mentions with a touch of regret: "When a man really makes a success of his life, ninety-nine percent of his friends vanish."[iii]

**The Mental Dimension (continual learning)**
Not part of the Wealth & Status map unless the purpose is to impress others.

**The Spiritual[13] Dimension (connections with religion, or art, or nature, or charity, etc.)**
Not part of the Wealth & Status map unless the purpose is to impress others.

In the board game Monopoly, the sole aim is summed up at the end of the directions: "RICHEST PLAYER WINS!" In Monopoly, there's no problem with wealth and status being the only measure of success. The board pieces derive no joy from maintaining close relationships with

---

[iii] Michael Korda, *Power! How to Get It, How to Use It*, p. 46. Interview with Robert Guccione, creator of *Penthouse*.

43

their spouses and children and friends, they don't need time for exercise or sufficient sleep, and they have no interest in music or art. The board pieces can "win" while excluding those aspects of life. Measuring success through wealth alone works well for a board game, but there are drawbacks to making it a model for real life. Psychotherapist Douglas LaBier's book *Modern Madness* is filled with stories from people who achieved this Monopoly-version of success, yet ended up disillusioned with it. Part of the package of making it "to the top," LaBier's patients often discovered, included suffering from unexplained physical ailments, anxiety, depression, rage, overuse of drugs and alcohol, distrustful relationships with their associates, and estrangement from their children and spouses.

I once read an article about a breast surgeon who, following the standard American version of success, strove hard for something that in the end made her unhappy.[iv] When she was one of the regular hospital staff surgeons, she seemed to have a rewarding and well-balanced life. Not only did she make a good salary and have the respect of others in her field, she also took pride in the compassionate care she gave her breast cancer patients, who often needed an enormous amount of counseling and support. But because she accepted society's goal of continually striving for more wealth and status, she gradually made her life miserable by moving "up" to the position of Chief of Breast Surgery. To convince the higher-ups she was worthy of the promotion, hospital politics demanded that she prove her money-making abilities—which meant doubling her fees, working twelve-hour shifts, and seeing up to forty patients a day. As she did so, she felt her nerves frazzling and the quality of her care diminishing. She even admitted that she wondered why she was pursuing something that was driving her crazy. She persisted nonetheless and won the position, but described her victory as demoralizing. In terms of wealth, status, and the "more is better" mindset, her new title was indeed a step up. But in terms of a happy life, everything in the article suggested to me that it was a step down: that she was far better off before her "promotion."

---

[iv] "The Hell of Having it All," *Vogue*, August 1995.

What does the phrase "That person's a success!" imply? In America, career success and happiness are understood to be one in the same. But you can have either without the other.

Yet although having a well-paying job comes with no guarantee of happiness, working nothing but minimum-wage jobs *is* almost guaranteed to come with a degree of suffering. Not being able to provide for your physical dimension also affects your emotional, mental, and spiritual dimensions: especially if you have a family and can't provide sufficient food, clothing, housing, and medical care. Plus there's the additional complication that having a minimum-wage job tends to mean that forty-plus hours of your week are spent doing dull and repetitive work. What I'm proposing here—and this is my main point for this *Measuring Success* chapter—is that the Four Dimensions map can be used as a guideline to avoid both the hollowness of a life focused on pursuing nothing but wealth and status, and the miseries that come with jobs that starve your bank account and numb your mind. I'm proposing that peace within employment rests in having a job that:

(1)   adequately supplies the financial subsection of your physical dimension (Chapter 5's *enough*), and

(2)   contributes to, or at least doesn't overly interfere with, your pursuit of achieving a satisfying balance of your emotional, mental, spiritual, and physical (the health subsection of sleep, diet, and exercise) dimensions.[v]

(I use the phrase "satisfying balance" rather than "fulfillment" because time constraints put the dimensions of our lives in competition with each other: we generally don't have all the time we'd like for our families *and* fitness *and* earning our salaries, and so on. But the Wealth & Status map doesn't give consideration to much else besides wealth and status; the Four Dimensions map gives a fair hearing to all the compartments of our lives.)

---

[v] As J. Bronowski writes in *The Ascent of Man:* "The good life is *more* than material decency, but the good life must be *based* on material decency" (p. 279).

In *Your Money or Your Life,* Dominguez and Robin approach the issue of balance by separating the terms *work* and *paid employment.* They redefine *work* as all our purposeful activities, and define *paid employment* as the particular activity that takes care of our economic needs. With that perspective, many followers of Dominguez and Robin's workshops decided to aim for the highest paying job they could: not for the materialistic "more is better" reason, but with the goal of working as few hours as were necessary to meet their financial requirements. Without the expectation that their paid employment was supposed to represent their meaning in life, they often found that those activities which *did* represent their meaning were best pursued when financial strings were not attached. Applied to the framework of balancing our four dimensions, *paid employment*'s only concern is the subsection of the physical requirement for money, whereas *work* is concerned with all four dimensions.

For some, a focus on wealth and status might be satisfying enough. An aggressive and childless entrepreneur may, for all I know, find complete emotional, mental, and spiritual satisfaction in carving out his or her own niche in the business world. I'm just saying that our culture's path of "happiness through career success" is not for everyone. The big question "What do you want to *be* when you grow up?" might be more appropriately phrased "What type of paid employment do you think will best complement your physical, emotional, mental, and spiritual dimensions?"

. . .

I'm hesitant to use my own life as an illustration of using the Four Dimensions map. This is partly because I have yet to achieve the balance I'm looking for, so my story may not be the best example. But because I also find that books such as these are more credible when the author includes the personal impact, I feel I need to include my experience.

Prior to parenthood, as mentioned in this book's introduction, I felt no significant conflicts in fully dedicating my life to my career as a musician (although in my case, career dedication was more about Work = Identity, rather than Work = a sure path to Wealth & Status). Upon becoming a father, however, my life became a poor balancing act between trying to support my new family, and continuing to struggle in the fiercely competitive music industry. Basically I was doing a half-assed job at both. Around the time of my son's first birthday, I was forced to reevaluate my career goals after I was lucky enough to get in a car accident that left me unable to walk for several months. I *do* mean lucky: the accident made me take a break from business as usual and reexamine my life—how my career choice was making me a distant father, a financially and emotionally unsupportive husband, and constantly stressed.

After deciding to put the professional pursuit of music on hold, my first attempt at reconciling the opposing forces of having a happy family life *and* a career by which I could define myself was to modify society's goal of wealth and status by trying to limit my career commitment to a forty-hour workweek. I learned to type, registered as an office temp, ended up getting a secretarial job in a large company, and kept on the lookout for promotions. After a couple years I worked my way into a position that gave me the mental stimulation and the bit of status I was looking for, and it had only occasional demands for traveling and for working beyond the usual nine to five. My position's salary had to be supplemented with waiting tables on the weekends, but the job promised future raises that would eventually allow me to give up those shifts.

My newly attained status (and hopes for large future raises) took a step backwards when a massive layoff wiped out my entire department. I managed to stay employed, but only by accepting a transfer—and a demotion—to a mindless data-entry slot. I hated the new position, and took it only as a way to bring in money while searching elsewhere for work. Two things, however, made me abandon this search. First, I discovered that my data-entry job's lack of demand for a brain meant that my mind was free to concentrate on listening to books on tape while I worked. Second, while working on the first draft of this book, I began to redefine the goal for my paid employment. Once I started to think of employment's purpose as fulfilling only a subsection of my physical dimension, while either complementing or not overly interfering with my other dimensions, my job didn't look all that bad anymore.

Not only did I stop looking for another position, I've since turned down several promotion offers, and have let my supervisors know that I'm not interested in any future advancements. My decision to stay where I am would make no sense if my goals were wealth and status—I'll never get rich, it's not a "career," and I have little status. But it *does* make sense when I measure my job by how well it contributes to a balanced life: it's compatible with raising children (no travel, no important meetings, no staying past 5:00 or bringing work home); it's educational because I get to listen to about fifty books a year (borrowed from a nearby library); it allows time for sleep and exercise; and, with the help of my seemingly eternal sentence as a weekend waiter, it financially provides for my household.

I admit that my solution is not ideal, as it still doesn't allow for all the time I'd like for music and writing. Switching my goal to aiming for a balance of my four dimensions, however, doesn't magically give me extra hours in the day. It just gives me the big picture of what my priorities are. And all things considered, my work arrangement is satisfactory, and the least stressful I've had since taking on the responsibilities of parenthood.[14]

Of course, if prior to parenthood I'd been a scientist on the verge of a great discovery, or a politician making important strides in world peace, or say a financially successful musician, I'm sure I would have ended up juggling things differently. A goal of balancing your four dimensions allows for a great deal of variety. And I'm certainly not suggesting that a dead end data-entry job and part-time waitering should fit anybody else's definition of a good balance: this just happens to be working well enough for me at this time in my life. Once my children gain their independence and my priorities shift, I suspect it will be time for me to move on. But regardless of what employment I look for in the years to come, I now have a more reliable guideline on which to base that decision.

# Closing

As someone who grew up with only a dim awareness of the world of work and finance, I plan on making sure my children are better prepared for what lies ahead when the time comes for them to venture out on their own. This doesn't mean I plan on offering them specific advice on which careers to choose; my responsibility as a parent is to provide not a path but only a lamppost, or better yet a lantern. And I'd like this lantern to illuminate the following:

First, in order to obtain their survival needs and all the extras—from food, clothing and shelter to antibiotics to videogames—some type of labor is required.

Second, if their tastes are simple enough, they may choose to find and live in a community where all their labor is directly linked to providing their survival basics (see endnote 10). If they choose to live in mainstream society, however, they'll have to accept the arrangement of working indirectly for their needs via specialized labor bartered through our medium-of-exchange.

Finally, if they base their career decisions on our culture's guideline of aiming for maximum wealth and status, they may discover years down the road that they're unhappy with the results, even if they arrive at the place where society promised fulfillment. If they rebel without direction, deciding that financial considerations should never have any influence in their pursuits, they may find themselves plagued with the stress that comes with poverty. If, however, they make their goal a balance of their physical, social, mental, and spiritual dimensions as they decide upon their work and their paid employment (whether or not these are one in the same), they'll have a greater chance of being at peace with both their work and their money.

# Endnotes

## CHAPTER ONE

[1] In economist Robert Frank's book *Luxury Fever,* he uses the example of bread-baking to demonstrate the efficiency of specialization versus the inefficiency of doing everything oneself:

> Although [this do-it-all-yourselfer claims] that "five hours to make a loaf of bread does not seem like a long time," it is in fact a *very* long time. Even a minimum-wage worker can buy a terrific loaf of fresh bread at the bakery near my house for less than she earns in 15 minutes. Professional bakers are simply much more efficient than the rest of us at making bread, and relying on them to perform that task frees us up to spend more time on things we are comparatively good at doing. My point is not that professional bakers should be the only ones ever to bake bread, but rather that baking your own bread makes sense only if you find the experience itself enjoyable relative to other uses of your time.

(*Luxury Fever*, pp. 190–191, © 1999 by Robert H. Frank. Reprinted by permission of Princeton University Press.)

[2] The larger populations made possible by the age of agriculture's increased food supply and stable living conditions also gave rise to new miseries. The "crowd epidemic" was one: instead of wiping out isolated hunting and gathering tribes and spreading no further, diseases such as smallpox, tuberculosis, and the bubonic plague could persist for centuries and kill millions. (This was particularly true in the crowded cities of Europe. Resistances to these diseases, built up by those who managed to survive the epidemics, later became a powerful weapon of the Europeans when they invaded other continents.) The division of labor caused new problems as well—a divided labor force gave a community the benefits of expert craftsmanship, but it also gave rise to class conflicts, slavery,

professional armies, and an increase in the frequency and severity of wars.


[3] An attempt at a more complete answer involves going off on a tangent from the focus on "why we have to work." In trying to keep to that focus, these tangent issues are being stuck back here in the endnotes.

Unlike agriculture, industry did not spring up independently in different continents. The Industrial Revolution started in England, spread rapidly throughout Europe and America, and then throughout the rest of the world. The question this endnote will attempt to answer is why the common task of obtaining food, clothing and shelter took so many different directions in different parts of the world—why did some people remain hunters and gatherers, others become farmers and herders, others develop complex villages and cities, and others develop industry? Did industry begin with the English because they were biologically more industrious and ingenious (as many of them at the time liked to believe), or more destructive and exploitative (as many others believed), or something else altogether?

According to the Encyclopedia Britannica (under *Work, Organization of*, subtopic *Theories of Civilization's Development*), the factors that lead to "civilization" are geography, climate, neighbors, and the types of available crops and animals. The following explains why crops and animals were so critical:

ANIMALS: Only a small number of animal species are suitable for domestication, as survival instincts such as flight reflex and territorial behavior make the taming of most animals impossible. Horses, cows, and yaks are among the few that will docilely work for humans to provide a steady source of farm power. For communities with such animals (and not every part of the world had an equal share), domestication reduced the number of people needed for food production, thus increasing the number of specialists in fields outside of food production. For communities *without* domesticatable animals—communities where the native wildlife was limited to those such as bison, zebras, and kangaroos (none of whom can be convinced to pull plows or otherwise help out on the farm)—laboring for one's food had to be done by great numbers of the population, thus restricting the number of specialists in other fields.

PLANTS: Similarly, not all edible plants are suitable for domestication. Only a relatively few can be domesticated to the point where large amounts can be easily planted, harvested, and stored (at least in pre-industrial times). And as with domesticatable animals, not every part of the world received an equal share. Wheat—native to the Middle East—for example, could be planted en mass by scattering, and harvested en mass with a sickle. Corn—native to the Americas—had to be planted by hand, the cobs had to be shucked, and the kernels had to be scraped. Comparing the two, wheat did a much better job at allowing great amounts of food to be produced by just a small number of laborers.

So those areas with access to easily domesticatable plants and animals ended up with a relatively small segment of the population feeding the rest, freeing the others to dedicate their time to specializing in skills such as science, metallurgy, and weaponry. Those areas without easily domesticatable plants and animals ended up with far fewer specialists. (Note: It's common to see images of Native Americans on horses, but those horses didn't arrive until the Europeans brought them.) The degree to which such resources were available helps to explain why the Australian aborigines remained hunters and gatherers, why most of the natives of Africa and North America mixed agriculture and specialized skills with hunting and gathering, why China and the Middle East were able to develop complex cities, and why Europe ended up with cities and industry.

(This endnote draws largely on Jared Diamond's essay "Accidental Conquerors," from his book *The Third Chimpanzee*.)

[4] The new methods of the Industrial Revolution spread rapidly not only throughout Europe and America, but throughout most other continents as well. Armed with modern weaponry and resistances to their own infectious diseases, Europeans managed to successfully invade and set up puppet governments all over the world. A main incentive for these invasions was to set up labor systems that would allow Europe to have cheap access to raw materials such as tin, oil, coal, rubber, and copper

for its factories. As a result, natives who were once self-sufficient in Africa, China, India, South America, etc. were forced into becoming units of this huge worldwide market.

Most colonized countries managed to free themselves of foreign control between the 1950s and 1970s, but the European economic systems that had been imposed for so long couldn't just disappear. These post-colonial nations couldn't all of a sudden go back to their "old ways," and the European withdrawals often just meant a change in the hands of ownership, not a change in economic structure. This helps to explain why our convoluted workday is so common around the world.

[5] I spoke at length with a homeless man about the ideas I was gathering for this book, and he disagreed that you needed either some sort of work or welfare to get your food, clothing and shelter. He also spoke a great deal about his upcoming movie projects and his cure for AIDS, so I should mention that I didn't find him to be particularly sane. His delusions notwithstanding, he did have practical and first-hand knowledge about how to survive without money:

FOOD: "Surpluses everywhere …" as long as you don't mind going through dumpsters near convenience stores. Wrapped sandwiches thrown out just because they had passed their sale date still tasted fine.

CLOTHES: The trick here was to go to clothing donation sites late at night. He said the nine to five donation hours were inconvenient for many people, so clothes were often just left in front of these stores after closing time.

SHELTER: This could sometimes be a problem, but for the time being he had managed to set up a relatively safe and dry campsite near an irrigation ditch. As far as hygiene goes, he stayed clean by using the showers at a nearby college, where he impersonated an employee.

But although he felt that his access to survival basics was "reliable," he did admit that the scavenging lifestyle has its unattractive aspects: without heat, his campsite could get quite cold in the winter; without a refrigerator, he had to search for food quite often (especially in the summer, when food spoiled quickly); and without an enclosed shelter, he had to deal with thieves and rodents (thieves would steal his winter blankets, and rats were a year-round problem). There were also occasional threats of violence due to competition from fellow dumpster-rooters, particularly on the day when his favorite convenience store discarded its popular cheese-steak sandwiches.

# CHAPTER TWO

[6] An efficient store-of-value permits large accumulations. One repercussion of this is the creation of a class of people who *don't* have to work, such as those who have accumulated or inherited vast sums and can live off the interest. For such people, the community's store-of-value allows them to trade continually with nothing but stored labor (whether it be labor of theirs or the labor of others). Arrangements like this are difficult to pull off in communities where the store-of-value is something perishable like wheat.

[7] Using a medium-of-exchange was the best way to get around bartering's limitations before the computer age, but today there are other options. The Internet makes it easier to find parties interested in mutual trade, thus reducing the *double coincidence of wants* problem; and databases make it easier to keep track of having multiple prices for a single good, thus reducing the need for money as a measure-of-value. In *The Third Wave*, Toffler discusses how we often make the mistake of using First Wave and Second Wave solutions when Third Wave technology would be more appropriate. In some instances this is applicable to the unnecessary use of money.

But this is not to say that using a medium-of-exchange is outdated: in most cases, using money is still a lot easier than having to rely on computers for establishing trading values and finding bartering partners.

# CHAPTER FOUR

[8] While I realize that Goodman's complaint about "turning away from subsistence jobs" refers to the way modern humans no longer have a hands-on connection with providing our food, clothing and shelter, I feel the need to comment that even jobs such as videogame programming *are* subsistence-providing: they add value to products that are used to trade (via our medium-of-exchange) with specialists from the food, clothing and shelter industries.

[9] Multiple other researchers have come to the same conclusion. The www.schwab.com article "Some Things Money Can't Buy" (17 May 2000), for example, cites a study called "Income, Consumption and Happiness" which concluded that the connection between income and happiness tends to level off once people rise above the poverty level. Going from *not* being able to afford shoes for your children to being *able* to afford shoes—this almost always correlates with an increase in happiness. Going from being able to afford decent shoes to making so much that your kids feel justified in arguing for buying the latest and most expensive model every few months—this does not necessarily correlate with increased happiness.

In the *New Yorker* article "No Satisfaction" (25 January 1999), the conclusion that money has a limited correlation with happiness is supported by the following four sources: (1) Tibor Scitovsky's book *The Joyless Economy*, which discusses how excesses in material goods fail to bring human contentment; (2) research from Richard Easterlin (an economist at the University of Southern California), who found that the overall happiness of Americans between the end of World War II and the mid-1970s had increased very little, even though income and spending had quadrupled in that same period; (3) Andrew Oswald, who published similar results in *The Economic Journal* for studies done between 1970 and 1990; and (4) Michael Argyle (an Oxford University experimental psychologist), whose research led him to conclude "money has little effect [on happiness], except at the lower end of the income scale."

In *Luxury Fever*, Robert Frank writes that there are two main reasons for this phenomenon. One is that the remarkable ability that humans have for adaptation to changed circumstances is a double-edged sword, applying to both losses and gains: that which allows us to overcome depression upon becoming a quadriplegic also allows us to lose appreciation for luxuries upon becoming surrounded by them. The second reason is that we evaluate our position in life not by how much we have and how comfortable it makes us, but by how much we have relative to those around us. Frank quotes author H. L. Mencken's definition of a rich man: "one who makes $100 a year more than his wife's sister's husband."

[10] For those who feel totally at odds with mainstream society and want to live closer to the land, there's always the option of trying to find a self-sustaining farming community to live in. At the time of this book's publication, my internet search under the phrase "Intentional Communities" came up with directories that list over 1,600 such groups (and this is only a partial list, as it includes only those with websites). The people in these communities usually number less than one hundred, and are dedicated to self-sufficiency: growing their own food, building their own shelters, creating their own mini-governments, digging their own outhouses, etc. Most of these communities welcome visitors who want to see if this route is the right one for them.

## CHAPTER FIVE

[11] Rather than glance at your paycheck to see how much you earn per hour, Dominguez and Robin recommend taking the following steps to figure out your "real" hourly wage:

*Step One*: Figure out the monthly cash equivalent of your job's benefits and add it to your monthly take-home pay.
Say your monthly take-home pay is $2,100 (a 35-hour week at $15/hour take-home). Say your benefits (health insurance, tuition

reimbursement, contributions to a retirement fund, etc.) add up to a cash equivalent of $13,440 per year, or $1,120 per month. This brings your monthly salary up to $3,220, or an hourly wage of $23.

*Step Two:* Add up all your monthly job-related expenses, and subtract that figure from your monthly salary.

*All* work-related expenses should be taken into account. Let's say that the expenses of clothes, transportation, the cost of the drink you need after work to relax, vacations to get away, and therapy because your job makes you crazy, all add up to $9,840 per year (or $820 per month that your job is *costing* you). Subtracting that $820 from your monthly salary of $3,220 brings it down to $2,400, or an hourly wage of $17.14.

*Step Three:* Divide the monthly salary from Step Two by the number of hours your job consumes.

*All* work-related demands on your time should be taken into account: time spent at home preparing for or worrying about your job, time getting ready for work, time commuting, the time it takes if you have to go to therapy or have an after-work drink, etc. Add all this up, and your 35-hour work week may turn out to consume, say, 60 hours a week. Divide the monthly salary you arrived at in Step Two ($2,400) by the monthly number of hours your job consumes (240), and your hourly wage is brought down to $10.00

[12] The ideal state of *enough* is having an investment so large that its monthly interest is greater than your monthly expenses: this frees you from paid employment altogether. A road map for this goal is outlined in *Your Money or Your Life*, which is why its subtitle is *Transforming Your Relationship with Money and Achieving Financial Independence*.

Regardless of how positive this goal may be, I've omitted its details from my book for two reasons: (1) I feel that such an arrangement requires having a larger investment and/or a thriftier lifestyle than is realistic for most of us, and (2) the 1992 *Your Money or Your Life* based its investment strategy on buying 30-year Treasury bonds, which at the time of the book's publication paid 7.5%, an unusually high interest rate.

# CHAPTER SIX

[13] The word *spiritual* means different things to different people:

- To those who follow traditional Western religions, spirituality has to do with one's relationship with God.

- To those who follow traditional Eastern religions, spirituality is generally used in reference to the aspect of divinity that's within one's self.

- To those drawn to more modern religious ideas, which for lack of a better term I'll call "New Age," spirituality is generally used in reference to a mysterious Higher Power that transcends the doctrines of organized religions. Beliefs about this Higher Power vary and may include any of the following:
  · the West-influenced idea of a monotheistic God that created everything, but is separate from His Creation;
  · the East-influenced idea of divinity as one universal substance that we are all a part of;
  · ancient throwback beliefs involving ancestor worship, or animism (the belief that everything in nature—whether person, plant, or cloud—has its own spirit), or polytheism (believing that there's a different god for every area of life: one for war, one for love, one for agriculture, etc.);
  · a vague mixture of some, or all, of the above.

- To many atheists and other nontheists, spirituality refers to the placebo effect that accompanies religious delusion and wishful thinking (although some nontheists use the word when referring to the sense of awe when being immersed in or overwhelmed with beauty, be it through art, music, nature, poetry, literature, special human relationships, etc.).

For the first three groups, the phrase "Spiritual Dimension" is clear enough. For nontheists, the wording is probably inappropriate, and if I really wanted to be all-inclusive, I would change the phrase to "Spiritual / Artistic / Creative / Aesthetic / Charitable / Etc. Dimension." But because I find this wordy and awkward, I'm just going to leave it as "Spiritual," and hope this endnote offers sufficient clarification.


[14] True, I *might* be able to make more time for music and writing if I had the ambition to get "further ahead" at the office and eliminate the need for a supplementary income from waiting tables. Moving "up," however, would most likely be even more intrusive than my waiting shifts: the extra responsibilities would make it harder to put my family first when it came to work vs. family conflicts, and if I had a job that required thinking, I wouldn't be able to listen to books on tape while I worked.

Given that I'd still like to improve my situation, my long-shot plan for replacing my restaurant income is to make money through publishing my writing (which I've previously circulated only among friends and family). Hardly a sure-fire strategy, but if you paid for the copy in your hands, then maybe it's working.

# References

Berg, Adriane G. *Your Wealth-Building Years—Financial Planning for 18- to 38-Year-Olds.* New York: Newmarket Press, 1992.

Berry, Wendell. *The Unsettling of America: Culture & Agriculture.* New York: Avon Books, 1977.

Bronowski, J. *The Ascent of Man.* Boston: Little, Brown and Company, 1973.

Cassidy, John. "No Satisfaction." *The New Yorker,* 25 January 1999.

Chantrell, Glynnis (editor). *The Oxford Dictionary of Word Histories.* New York: Oxford University Press, 2002.

Collodi, Carlo. *Pinocchio.* 1880. Morris Plains, NJ: The Unicorn Publishing House, 1986.

Covey, Stephen R. *The 7 Habits of Highly Effective People.* New York: Simon & Schuster, 1989.

Crosby, Alfred W. *Ecological Imperialism.* New York: Cambridge University Press, 1986.

Davidow, William. "Does Money Exist?" *Forbes ASAP,* 3 June 1996.

Defoe, Daniel. *Robinson Crusoe.* 1719. New York: Penguin Putnam, Inc., 2001.

Diamond, Jared. *The Third Chimpanzee: The Evolution and Future of the Human Animal.* New York: HarperCollins Publishers, Inc., 1992.

Dominguez, Joe and Vicki Robin. *Your Money or Your Life: Transforming Your Relationship with Money and Achieving Financial Independence.* New York: Penguin Books, 1992.

Frank, Robert. *Luxury Fever: Why Money Fails to Satisfy in an Era of Excess.* Princeton: Princeton University Press, 2000.

Gogh, Vincent Van. *The Letters of Vincent Van Gogh.* 1886–1890. Edited by Mark Roskill. New York: Atheneum, 1963.

Goodman, Paul. *Growing Up Absurd.* New York: Vintage Books, 1956.

Gould, Stephen Jay. *Bully for Brontosaurus.* New York: Norton, 1991.

Gould, Stephen Jay. *Ever Since Darwin.* New York: W. W. Norton & Company, 1992.

Gould, Stephen Jay. *Full House.* New York: Harmony Books, 1996.

Green, Stephanie. "Some Things Money Can't Buy." Article on www.schwab.com, 17 May 2000 (a report on Aaron Ahuvia's study "Income, Consumption and Happiness").

Korda, Michael. *Power! How to Get It, How to Use It.* New York: Ballantine Books, 1975.

LaBier, Douglas. *Modern Madness.* Boston: Addison-Wesley Publishing Co., 1986.

Marx, Karl and Friedrich Engels. *The Communist Manifesto.* 1848. New York: Oxford University Press, 1998.

Mundis, Jerrold. *How to Get Out of Debt, Stay Out of Debt, and Live Prosperously.* New York: Bantam Books, 1990.

Pringle, Heather. "The Cradle of Cash." *Discover Magazine,* October 1998.

Spencer, Milton H. and Orley M. Amos, Jr. *Contemporary Macroeconomics.* New York: Worth Publishers, 1993.

Terkel, Studs. *Working.* New York: Ballantine Books, 1974.

*The New Encyclopaedia Britannica.* Chicago: Encyclopaedia Britannica, Inc., 1980.
  *Agriculture, History of*
  *Alienation of Labor*
  *Colonialism*
  *Economic History, The Industrial Revolution*
  *Europe, Plant and Animal Life*
  *Instrumentation, History*
  *Money*
  *Work, Organization of*

Thoreau, Henry David. *Walden and Other Writings.* 1854. Edited by Joseph Wood Krutch. New York: Bantam Classic, 1981.

Toffler, Alvin. *Previews and Premises.* Cambridge, MA: South End Press, 1984.

Toffler, Alvin. *The Third Wave.* New York: William Morrow and Company, Inc., 1980.

Voltaire, Francois. *Candide.* 1759. Translation by Lowell Bair. New York: Bantam Books Inc., 1984.

Walsh, Elsa. "The Hell of Having it All." *Vogue,* August 1995.

Weatherford, Jack. *Savages and Civilization.* New York: Ballantine Books, 1994.

# Index

# About the Author

My first career, and my BA from Queens College, was in music. I spent the early 1980s working miscellaneous jobs around New York City (playing piano for dance classes, cable television, Off-Off Broadway shows); left the city for several years to play keyboards and blues harp in road bands; and in the mid-1980s returned to New York to play in a number of pretentious rock-star-wannabe bands (and most of all, to wait tables). In the late 1980s I got married and started a family, and since the 1990s I've been working an office job and playing piano and guitar for my children's grade school.

I live with my wife, daughter, and three sons in Brooklyn, New York.

. . .

Also by Todd Allen Gates: *Dialogue with a Christian Proselytizer.*

ingramcontent.com/pod-product-compliance
Source LLC
burg PA
28290526
2003B/1439